"All that is gold does not glitter, not all those who wander are lost; the old that is strong does not wither, deep roots are not reached by the frost."

Preface

Greetings, fellow adventurer! Welcome to a hidden corner of Middle-earth, where languages whisper of ancient lore and forgotten times. This humble tome shall be your guide to three of the world's most fascinating and veiled tongues: Noldorin, Rohirric, and the Black Speech.

Within these pages, you'll find a treasure trove of words, each carrying the weight of J.R.R. Tolkien's meticulous imagination. From the silver grace of Noldorin, the tongue of the Firstborn, to the hearty strength of Rohirric, spoken by the proud Riders of the Mark, each word offers a glimpse into the cultures and peoples that brought them forth.

But delve deeper, brave soul, and you will encounter the chilling power of the Black Speech, a language forged for darkness and dominion. Its harsh syllables echo with the shadows of Mordor, and its very essence sends shivers down the spine.

So, open your mind, and let the languages of Tolkien guide you. May your path be filled with wonder, and may your understanding of his world be forever deepened.

Onward, and may the words light your way!

Table of Contents

Noldorin

History

A Celtic-sounding language spoken by the Gnomes/Noldoli existed since the beginning of Tolkien's mythology. In its first stages it was called Gnomish and resembled the later Noldorin/Sindarin despite noticeable differences.

The evolution of the language continued over several years. During the 1930s it was known as Noldorin and gained a greater similarity to the Sindarin of The Lord of the Rings. This version of the language appears in the Etymologies.

Noldorin was the existing version of the language during the writing of The Lord of the Rings. The Elvish phrases in The Lord of the Rings, now known as Sindarin, were "Noldorin" in Tolkien's mind throughout the writing process. It was only while compiling the Appendices that he decided to rewrite the language's back-story and change the name to Sindarin.

Tolkien consulted the Noldorin language of the Etymologies extensively in his work on Sindarin, adapting old words to fit his new version of the language. This same method of adapting Noldorin words to create Sindarin equivalents is used by modern students of Elvish. The resulting vocabulary is typically referred to as "Neo-Sindarin" to distinguish it from attested Sindarin.

In the books...

Kornoldorin ("Gnomish of Kôr" or "Old Noldorin") was the language of the Gnomes in Valinor. It was similar to Qenya, the language of the Lindar, but incorporated Solosimpin influence.

When the Noldoli came to the Great Lands with Fëanor, they intermingled with the Ilkorindi, the Dark Elves, and their languages, Kornoldorin and Ilkorin respectively, were likewise mingled. This was the origin of Noldorin.

Noldorin was rich in various dialects, including those of Mithrim, Gondolin, Nargothrond, and Himring and the Fëanorian dialect of East Beleriand spoken by the folk of the Sons of Fëanor.

A

agr: narrow (adjective)

alf: swan (noun)

ambar: world, Earth (noun)

amben: uphill, sloping upwards (adverb)

ambend: uphill, sloping upwards (adverb)

ammarth: fate, doom (noun)

andabon: elephant (noun)

andeith: long mark (noun)

anrand: age, 100 Valian years (noun)

anw: male (adjective)

ar-: high, noble, royal (prepostional/adjectival/adverbial prefix)

arnoediad: very large in number, countless, innumerable (adjective)

ascar: violent, impetuous (Sindarin, adjective)

atlant: oblique (adjective)

B

bann: prison, custody (noun)

bein: beautiful, fair (adjective)

belt: strong, especially in body (adjective)

berein: trusty men (noun)

besain: bread giver (noun)

besoneth: bread giver (noun)

brann: 1.lofty, noble, fine 2.high (in size) (adjective)

brethel: beech or silver birch tree (noun)

bui: (it is) necessary (to), one needs (to) (fixed expression)

bunn: 1.long projecting or anterior elongation of an animal's head; especially the nose (noun) 2.a strip of land projecting into a body of water, cape (noun)

C

cabr: frog (noun)

cadw: shaped, formed (adjective)

cadwar: having a well-proportioned and pleasing shape(adjective)

calf: water-vessel (noun)

camb: hand (noun)

camland: palm of hand (noun)

camm: hand (noun)

cann: bold (adjective)

ceir: ship (noun)

celefn: made of silver (adjective)

celeir: brilliant (adjective)

celw: source, spring (of water) (noun)

chwand: fungus, sponge (noun)

chwest: a slight and short movement of the air, breath, puff (noun)

chwîn: dizziness, faintness (noun)

chwind: twirling, whirling (adjective)

chwiniol: twirling, whirling (verb)

cirban: haven (noun)

coe: earth, ground (noun)

corw: cunning, wily (adjective)

cramb: cake of compressed flour, often containing honey and milk (noun)

cumb: mound, heap (noun)

cunn: prince (noun)

cúran: the crescent moon (noun)

curw: craft, skill (noun)

D

dadben: downhill, inclined, prone (adjective)

dagr: battle (noun)

deloth: annoyance, abhorrence, detestation, loathing(

noun)

delw: hateful, deadly, fell (adjective)

doer: bridegroom (noun)

dolt: 1.dark, dusky, obscure (adjective) 2.round knob,

boss (noun)

dramb: heavy stroke, a blow (noun)

dramm: heavy stroke, a blow (noun)

dúlin: nightingale (noun)

dúlind: nightingale (noun)

dúwath: shadow, darkness, nightshade (noun)

E

echuiw: awakening (noun)

edeb: buildings, houses (noun)

edeir: fathers (noun)

edinar: birthday, anniversary day (noun)

edrein: border (noun)

egthel: point of spear (noun)

eilian: rainbow (noun)

eilianw: rainbow (noun)

eirch: orcs (noun)

elw: pale blue (adjective)

emelin: yellow small bird (noun)

emmelin: yellow small bird (noun)

emuin: hills (noun)

erch: orcs (noun)

F

fein: white (adjective)

feir: 1.mortal (noun) 2.right hand (noun)

feles: shores, beaches (noun)

fend: threshold, door (noun)

fenn: threshold, door (noun)

find: tress (noun)

findel: tress (noun)

finn: tress (noun)

fliw: sickness (noun)

floss: whisper, rustling sound (noun)

foeg: mean, poor, bad (adjective)

foen: radiant, beamy (adjective)

forodweith: northmen (noun)

G

gadr: prison, dungeon (verb)

gaeron: great sea, ocean (noun)

gail: brilliant light (noun)

galw: blessing, good fortune (noun)

gaw-: to howl (verb)

glambr: echo (noun)

glas: joy (noun)

glînn: gleam, especially of the eyes (noun)

glintha-: to glance at (verb)

glor: golden light (of the tree Laurelin) (noun)

godrebh: through together (adverb)

goer: red, copper coloured (adjective)

gonn: great stone, rock (noun)

graug: a demon, an evil creature (noun)

guin: goose (noun)

gwanw: death, as an action not a state (noun)

gwelw: air, as a substance (noun)

gwend: bound (verb) past tense

gwenn: 1.maiden, girl (noun) 2.bound (verb) past tense of the verb gwedhi

H

haglath: sling, slingshot (noun)

hana: it (pronoun)

hann: intelligent, clever (adjective)

harw: wound (noun)

hathel: 1.blade, esp. a large one, as of an axe (noun)

2.axe (noun)

hebeid: shores, coasts (noun)

hein: they, them (pronoun)

heir: 1.left hand (noun) 2.left (adjective)

heledirn: kingfisher bird (noun)

hend: eyed, with eyes (adjective)

hene: she (pronoun)

hethw: foggy, obscure (adjective)

hithw: mist, fog (noun)

hmael: 1.stain (noun) 2.stained (adjective)

hmaes: soil, stain (noun)

hniof: noose (noun)

hon: he (pronoun)

hono: he (pronoun)

huin: he (they)(pronoun)

I

idher: thoughtfulness (noun)

idhrin: year (noun)

idhrind: year (noun)

ifant: aged, long-lived (adjective)

inn: meaning (noun)

inw: female (adjective)

iolf: a brand (noun)

iond: son (noun)

ionn: son (noun)

iôr: course (noun)

L

lachend: an elf of Noldor (noun)

laegeldrim: green elves (noun)

lechind: elves of Noldor (noun)

lenn: journey (noun)

lhach: flickering flame (noun)

lhaden: open, clear (adjective)

lhaeg: keen, sharp, acute (adjective)

lhaes: baby (noun)

lhâf: (he/she) licks (verb)

lhagr: swift, fast (adjective)

lhain: free, freed (adjective)

lhalorn: elm-tree (noun)

lhalwen: elm-tree (noun)

lham: (physical) tongue (noun)

lhamb: (physical) tongue (noun)

lhammas: account of tongues (noun)

lhanc: throat (noun)

lhand: 1.open space (noun) 2.wide, broad (adjective)

lhang: sword (noun)

lhann: wide, broad (adjective)

lhant: a clearing (in a forest) (noun)

lhasbelin: autumm (noun)

lhass: leaf (noun)

lhathrado: eavesdrop (verb)

lhathron: eavesdropper, listener (noun)

lhaug: warm (adjective)

lhaws: hair ringlet (noun)

lhebed: finger (noun)

lheben: five (cardinal number)

lhedin: open, clear (adjective)

lhefneg: fifth (ordinal number)

lhein: free, freed (adjective)

lheithian: freedom, freeing from commitment or bondage(noun)

lheitho: to release (verb) infinitive

lhend: melodious, a pleasing tune (adjective)

lhim: fish (noun)

lhimb: fish (noun)

lhimlug: sea-serpent (compound noun)

lhimmint: moistened (verb) past tense

lhimp: wet (adjective)

lhîn: 1.) thin, meagre (adjective) plural of lhain 2.) pool (noun)

lhinn: tune (noun)

lhîr: row, range (noun)

lhoch: ringlet, a lock of hair (noun)

lhoeb: fresh (adjective)

lhong: heavy (adjective)

lhonn: narrow path (noun)

lhum: shade (noun)

lhumren: shady (adjective)

lhunt: boat (noun)

lhûth: spell, charm (noun)

lhútha-: to enchant, to cast a spell (verb)

lonn: narrow path, haven (noun)

M

magl: sword (noun)

malt: gold (the metal) (noun)

malw: pale, fallow (adjective)

megli: a bear, "honey-eater" (noun)

meglin: bear-like (adjective)

meidh: 1.pale, fawn (adjective) 2.fallow (adjective)

meil: pollen (noun)

mely: pollen (noun)

mesc: wet (adjective)

minei: single, distinct, unique (adjective)

minnas: tower (noun)

mistrad: 1.straying, wandering (verb) gerund 2.error

moed: handy, skilled (adjective)

moel: lust (noun)

moelui: lustful (adjective)

N

nand: 1.wide grassy land 2.grassy valley (noun)

nann: 1.wide grassy land 2.grassy valley (noun)

narw: red (adjective)

naugl: a dwarf (noun)

nedhw: cushion (noun)

neledh: three (cardinal number)

neledhi: to enter (verb)

neleg: tooth (noun)

nemb: nose (noun)

neweig: dwarves (noun)

nifred: pallor (noun)

nifredil: snowdrop flower (noun)

nim: white (adj)

no: under (preposition)

noer: sad, distressing, unhappy, lamentable (adjective)

nos: family, kindred, clan (noun)

nud-: to tie, to bind (verb)

nui: ideas (noun)

O

oear: sea (noun)

oegas: mountain top (noun)

oeges: mountain tops (noun)

oeglir: range of mountain tops (noun)

oel: lake, pool (noun)

oelin: lakes, pools (noun)

oer: sea (noun)

oeruil: seaweed (noun)

ofr: abundant (adjective)

old: violently fast stream of water, esp. coming from a mountain (noun)

ostrad: street (noun)

othlon: paved path, paved road (noun)

othlond: paved path, paved road (noun)

othrond: underground city (noun)

ovr: abundant (adjective)

P

pannod: fill (verb)

pathw: level space (noun)

peich: juice, syrup (noun)

pein: fixed boards, especially on the floor (noun)

penn: declivity (noun)

penninar: last day of the year (noun)

pichen: juicy (adjective)

R

rhaen: crooked (adjective)

rhaew: fathom, 6 feet for water depth (noun)

rhafn: an extended point at one side, similar to a horn(noun)

rhain: border, edge (noun)

rham: wall (noun)

rhamb: wall (noun)

rhanc: arm (noun)

rhandir: (masc) pilgrim, wanderer (noun)

rhasg: horn, especially of living animals (noun)

rhaud: metal (noun)

rhaudh: hollow (adjective)

rhaug: a demon, an evil creature (noun)

rhaun: errant, error-prone (adjective)

rhedhi: sow (verb) infinitive

rhein: 1.border, edge (noun) 2.footprint, track (noun)

rhem: frequent, numerous (adjective)

rhemb: frequent, numerous (adjective)

rhenc: arms (noun)

rhenio: stray (verb) infinitive

rhess: ravine, deep narrow steep-sided valley (noun)

rhest: cut (noun)

rhevio: 1.fly 2.sail 3.wander (verb) infinitive

rhibi: to scratch (verb)

rhien: 1.crowned (adjective) 2.queen (noun)

rhîf: edge, border (noun)

rhim: 1.a great number, a host (noun and suffix) 2.cold pool or lake, especially on the mountains (noun)

rhimb: 1.a great number, a host (noun and suffix) 2.cold pool or lake, especially on the mountains (noun)

rhîn: 1.crowned (adjective) 2.queen (noun)

rhind: circle (Sindarin, noun)

rhinn: 1.circular (adjective) 2.circle (noun)

rhîs: queen (noun)

rhis: ravine, deep narrow steep-sided valley (noun)

rhisto: 1.cut 2.rip (verb) infinitive

rhitho: to jerk, to move suddenly (verb) infinitive

rhoeg: bent, crooked (adjective)

rhofal: 1.wing 2.large feather (esp. of wings) (noun)

rhofel: 1.wings 2.large feathers (esp. of wings) (noun)

rhom: trumpet (noun)

rhomru: the sound of trumpets (noun)

rhond: cave or chamber with arch-shaped roof and not visible from outside (noun)

rhonn: cave or chamber with arch-shaped roof and not visible from outside (noun)

rhosc: brown (adjective)

rhû: loud sound (noun)

rhufen: East (noun)

rhui: 1.hunt, hunting (noun) 2.lions (noun) plural of rhaw

rhuiw: hunt, hunting (noun)

S

salf: soup (noun)

sein: new (adjective)

seleb: herbs (noun)

sui: juices (noun)

sûth: draught, a current of cold air (noun)

T

tachl: pin, brooch (noun)

tafr: woodpecker (noun)

talagand: harper (noun)

tar-: tough, stiff (adjective prefix)

tars: task (noun)

tathor: willow tree (noun)

tavr: woodpecker (noun)

tegl: pen (noun)

teil: feet, legs (noun)

teilia-: to play (verb)

teilien: sport, game, play (noun)

teilio: play (verb)

teith: mark (noun)

teleif: grounds, floors (noun)

tellein: sole (of a foot) (noun)

terein: brothers (noun)

thamb: hall (noun)

thambas: great hall (noun)

thaun: pine tree (noun)

therein: eagles (noun)

thinn: grey (adjective)

thlê: 1.very fine string or cord (noun) 2.spider filament (noun)

thlein: thin, meagre (adjective)

thlîn: thin, meagre (adjective)

thlind: fine, slender (adjective)

thling: spider, spider's web (noun)

thlingril: spider (noun)

thlinn: fine, slender (adjective)

thliw: sickness (noun)

thloss: whisper, rustling sound (noun)

thribi: to scratch (verb)

thross: whisper, rustling sound (noun)

tild: sharp point (noun)

tindu: twilight, dusk (noun)

tinw: small star (noun)

toll: island, isle (noun)

tonn: tall (adjective)

trener: recounted, narrated, told (verb)

tui: 1.sprout 2.partially opened flower (noun)

tuilin: swallow, small long-winged songbird (noun)

tuilind: swallow, small long-winged songbird (noun)

tunn: mound (noun)

U

uidavnen: ever-closed, ever-blocked (noun)

ulun: hideous creature, monster (noun)

ulund: hideous creature, monster (noun)

Rohirric

History

In the fictional world of Middle-earth by J. R. R. Tolkien, Rohirric is the language of the Rohirrim of Rohan.

In the novels it is always represented by Anglo-Saxon. This is because Tolkien saw the relationship between Rohirric and the Common Speech. to be the same as that of Anglo-Saxon and English, which was used to represent Westron. Only a few actual Rohirric words are given by Tolkien: kûd-dûkan, an old word meaning "hole-dweller" which led to kuduk, the name the Hobbits had for themselves. Even these terms were translated in the book: "hobbit" is said to derive from the Anglo-Saxon word Holbytla, or hole-builder.

The languages of the Kingdom of Rhovanion, Esgaroth and Dale (often called Dalish or Dale-ish) were related to Rohirric.

A

Aldor: Aldor (noun) literally ..... elder, chief. Aldor was the name of a king of Rohan who lived to a great age.

aldor: elder, chief (noun) (OE)

anborn: only-born, only-begotten (adj) (OE)

arod: quick, swift, ready (adj) (OE)

B

baldor: 1.) more bold, courageous, honorable (adj) (OE)

2.) prince, ruler (noun) (OE)

bema: trumpet (noun) (OE)

Béma: trumpet (noun) This was the name in Rohan for the Vala Oromë.

bisig: busy

bletsung: blessing, boon (noun)

Brand: 1.) firebrand (noun) 2.) torch (noun) Brand was the name of a King of Dale.

brytta: bestower, dispenser, distributor (noun) (OE)

burg: hill (noun)

C

ceorl: a freeman of the lowest class, churl, husbandman (noun) (OE)

coomb: narrow valley, deep hollow (noun) (Celtic)

cwén: queen (noun)

D

déor: 1.) deer, wild animal (noun) OE) 2.) brave or bold as a wild beast (adj) (OE)

deorwine: deer-friend, friend of wild animals (noun) (OE)

derndingle: secret (noun) (OE) + dell (noun) (ME) literally...the hollow where Entmoots were held

dernhelm: secret helmet, helmet of secrecy (noun) (OE)

dohtor: daughter (noun)

dunharg: hill temple (noun) (OE)

dunharrow: hill temple (noun) (OE)

dúnhere: hill warrior (noun) (OE)

dunland: hill-land, down-land (noun) (OE)

dunlending: hill-land, down-land (noun) (OE)

dwimmerlaik: legerdemain (noun) (ME) literally...'a trick of Sauron's magic'

dwimorberg: haunted mountain, mountain of phantoms (noun) (OE)

dwimordene: valley of illusion (noun) (OE)

E

eastemnet: east plain (noun) (OE)

eastfold: east earth (noun) (OE)

edoras: dwellings, places enclosed by a barrier (noun) (OE)

elfhelm: elf helmet (noun) (OE)

elfwine: elf-friend (noun) (OE)

ent: giant (noun) (OE)

éomer: horse mare (noun) (OE)

éomund: horse hand (noun) (OE)

éored: cavalry (noun) (OE)

éothain: horse thane (noun) (OE)

éothéod: horse folk (noun) (OE)

éowyn: one who delights in horses (adj) (OE)

erkenbrand: chief torch (noun) (OE)

F

feldland: plain-land (noun) (OE)

G

giest: guest (noun)

H

heo: she (pronoun)

hwít: white (adjective)

L

léoma: light (noun)

M

mægden: girl, maiden (noun)

móna: moon (noun)

Mundburg: OE compound meaning "sheltering hill". Mundburg was the Rohirric word for Minas Tirith (beneath Mindolluin)

O

orc: The word 'orc' appears in OE glosses from around AD 800, meaning 'demon' or 'ogre'; the word 'orcneas' meaning 'monsters' appears in the poem Beowulf. Both ultimately derive from the Latin 'Orcus'. who was a god of the underworld.

S

silfren: silver (noun)

simbelmynë: Evermind (noun) .... the small white flower

that grew especially on the graves of men

steorra: star (noun)

sweord: sword (noun)

W

wyn-: joy (prefix)

Black Speech

History

The Black Speech is one of the fictional languages constructed by J. R. R. Tolkien for his legendarium, where it was spoken in the evil realm of Mordor. In the fiction, Tolkien describes the language as created by Sauron as a constructed language to be the sole language of all the servants of Mordor.

Little is known of the Black Speech except the inscription on the One Ring. Scholars note that Tolkien constructed this to be plausible linguistically, and to sound rough and harsh. The scholar Alexandre Nemirovski, on linguistic evidence, has proposed that Tolkien based it on the ancient Hurrian language, which like the Black Speech was agglutinative.

-

-I: the (suffix)

-ish: in (postposition, suffix)

-uk: all (suffix)

-ul: them (pronoun)

-um: -ness (suffix)

A

agh: and (conjunction)

ash: one (cardinal number)

B

bagronk: cesspool (noun)

búbhosh: great (adjective)

búrz: dark (adjective)

burzum: darkness (noun)

D

dug: filth (noun)

durb-: rule (verb)

G

ghâsh: fire (noun)

gimb-: find (verb)

glob: fool (noun)

gûl: servant of Sauron (noun)...literally: a major, invisible servant of Sauron dominated entirely by his will

H

hai: folk (noun)

I

ishi: in the (postposition, suffix)

K

krimp-: bind (verb)

L

lug: tower (noun)

N

nazg: ring (noun)

Nazgûl: Ring-wraith (noun)...plural: Nazgûl

O

olog: troll (noun) literally: a troll of a kind developed by

Sauron

R

ronk: pool (noun)

S

sha: (interjection) an exclamation of contempt

sharkû: old man (noun)

skai: (interjection) an exclamation of contempt

snaga: slave (noun)

T

tark: man of Gondor (noun)

thrak-: bring (verb)

U

u: to (preposition)

uruk: orc (noun) literally: one of a great variety of orc

Printed in Great Britain
by Amazon